HUGH HUGHES PRESENTS SHÔN DALE-JONES IN

THE DUKE

produced by Hoipolloi, PBJ Management and Theatre Royal
Plymouth in association with Save The Children

OBERON BOOKS
LONDON

WWW.OBERONBOOKS.COM

First published in 2016 by Oberon Books Ltd
521 Caledonian Road, London N7 9RH
Tel: +44 (0) 20 7607 3637 / Fax: +44 (0) 20 7607 3629
e-mail: info@oberonbooks.com
www.oberonbooks.com

A catalogue record for this book is available from the British Library.

PB ISBN: 9781786820310
E ISBN: 9781786820327

Cover: photo by Jaimie Gramston; design by Stefanie Mueller

Printed, bound and converted
by CPI Group (UK) Ltd, Croydon, CR0 4YY.

Visit www.oberonbooks.com to read more about all our books and to buy them. You will also find features, author interviews and news of any author events, and you can sign up for e-newsletters so that you're always first to hear about our new releases.

Special thanks to:
Steffi Mueller; Josie Dale-Jones; Alex Byrne;
Gwen Dale-Jones; all past Hoipolloi Board members

Thanks to:
Toni Tippet: Nancy Poole: Anthony Alderson and the
team at Pleasance; Charmaine Wilson and team at
Salvation Army, Cambridge; Tania Harrison and team
at Latitude Festival; Ben Lloyd, Gemma Bodinetz and
team at Everyman, Liverpool; Nicky Webb; all the
partners we have ever worked alongside;
Lucy Davies, Hamish Pirie and team at Royal Court;
Purni Morell and team at Unicorn; Peter Bennett-Jones,
Kate Haldane and PBJ Management; Simon Stokes
and team at Theatre Royal Plymouth; Daniel Brine,
Daniel Pitt and team at Cambridge Junction;
Cathy Moore and team at Cambridge Literary Festival;
Simon Dodd; Robert Ziegler; Beverly Kirk,
Alisdair Roxburgh and team at Save The Children;
Sarah Evans and David Kefford from Aid & Abet;
Steve Marmion and team at Soho Theatre; Toni
Racklin and team at Barbican; The Team at Oberon
Books; Claudia West at Arts Council England

I'd like to dedicate this publication to everyone I've
ever collaborated and worked with at Hoipolloi.

A bit about Hoipolloi
and Shôn Dale-Jones

Hoipolloi makes the work of Artistic Director, Shôn Dale-Jones.

Hoipolloi connects with audiences nationally and internationally by sharing original comic stories, mixing fantasy and reality, making people laugh, cry and imagine.

Since co-founding the company with Stefanie Mueller in 1993, Shôn has worked as a writer, director, performer and producer, making over twenty new live theatre and comedy shows, as well as making work on radio, on screen and online. He is best known for his award-winning comic creation, Hugh Hughes and his hit shows *Floating, Story of a Rabbit, 360, Stories From An Invisible Town* and *Things I Forgot I Remembered*

Hoipolloi is a flexible and agile independent creative company, changing shape and size according to the scale and needs of each project. The company has worked with various partners, including the BBC; National Theatre Wales; National Theatre Studios; Barbican; Carriageworks, Sydney; Cambridge Film Festival; Arts Council England, The British Council.

Hoipolloi have performed all over London (Barbican, Roundhouse, BAC, Young Vic, Royal Opera House, Unicorn, Soho Theatre, Royal Court); nationally (including Liverpool, Everyman; Cambridge Junction; New Wolsey, Ipswich; West Yorkshire Playhouse; Northern Stage; Theatre Royal, Plymouth; Brighton Festival); the Edinburgh Festival Fringe (Assembly Rooms, Traverse Theatre, Pleasance) and internationally to Australia, Belgium, Canada, Colombia, Czech Republic, Finland, France, Germany, Holland, Ireland, Norway, The Philippines, Romania, Russia, Singapore, Sweden and the USA (including Sydney Opera House; Meyerhold Theatre, Moscow; Harbourfront Centre, Toronto; Barrow Street Theatre, New York; UCLA; Walker Arts Centre, Minneapolis; Push Festival, Vancouver; Dublin Theatre Festival; National Museum, Singapore)

Hoipolloi have won various awards, including a Scotsman Fringe First Award, Total Theatre Award, M-ie Award – Best Live Theatre Event, Melbourne, Australia and BBC Audio Drama Award for Best Scripted Comedy.

Hoipolloi 2016:

Artistic Director:	Shôn Dale-Jones
Associate Director:	Stefanie Mueller
Producer:	Jo Diver
Board of Directors:	Becky Schutt (Chair)
	David Sabel
	Hendrik McDermott

Press reviews for Hugh Hughes shows

Reviews of *Floating* include:

Hugh Hughes is a mesmerising personality…It's an extraordinary sight, hilarious yet touching in the human fragility it conveys…brilliantly effective in its simplicity
The Guardian ★ ★ ★ ★

Charming, surreal, warm-hearted…a piece of genius
The Scotsman ★ ★ ★ ★

Reviews of *Story of a Rabbit* include:

Hughes should be prescribed as medicine for depressives *Metro* ★ ★ ★ ★

This is heartfelt and insightful stuff that has great power to move. Highly recommended
Evening Standard ★ ★ ★ ★

Reviews of *360* include:

delightfully daft…warmly optimistic
Metro ★ ★ ★ ★

One of the most magical journeys
Financial Times ★ ★ ★ ★

Reviews of *Stories From An Invisible Town* include:

This is an inspiring, entertaining evening, full of underlying truths about what it is to be human.
Telegraph ★ ★ ★ ★

highly intelligent, beautifully performed…like Hughes's previous shows, this is a highly intelligent, beautifully performed piece that tugs the heartstrings with apparent real-life revelation, while spinning a story that's every bit as craftily constructed as a 'nice, well-written play'.
Time Out ★ ★ ★ ★

Reviews of *Things I Forgot I Remembered* include:

his recollections has a poignancy that takes you by surprise
The Guardian ★ ★ ★ ★

PBJ Management is proud to represent the brilliant Shôn-Dale Jones.

"I first first saw the great storyteller Shôn Dale-Jones in the guise of his comic creation Hugh Hughes at the Edinburgh Festival back in 2006. I was immediately enchanted by this comedic Welsh wizard and wanted to know more about this special, original artist. I linked him up with my Liverpool-based colleague, Kate Haldane, to help further his theatrical and filmic exploits." *Peter Bennett-Jones*

PBJ Management has been representing leading comedians, writer-performers and presenters for 30 years, including Lenny Henry, Rowan Atkinson, Tim Minchin, Eddie Izzard , Armando Iannucci, The Mighty Boosh, Nina Conti, The League of Gentlemen, Sally Phillips, Chris Morris, Alexander Armstrong , Gemma Whelan, Barry Humphries, Richard Ayoade and many more talented folk.

PBJ Management: Peter Bennett-Jones, Caroline Chignell (MD) , Kate Haldane, Dave Harries, Lucy Fairney, Emily Rees Jones, Janie Jenkins, Claire Nightingale, Patrick Bustin, Rebecca Ptaszynski, Dana Ondrejmiskova, Alice Burridge, Marina Campbell Grey, Paulene Tann, George Dent, Cathy Mason, Rachel Mason, Janette Linden, Clare Wilde, Jenny Rhodes, Daisy Skepelhorn, Rowan van den Berg, Suzanne Milligan and a special thank you to Toni Tippett for her work on this fine show.

Peter Bennett-Jones (founder of PBJ Management)

Peter is UK Chairman of Save the Children and is delighted by the charity's and PBJ Management's association with the production of *The Duke.*

"I have long been an admirer of and supporter of the excellent Shôn Dale Jones and his colleague, the incomparable Hugh Hughes. The Theatre Royal Plymouth has presented in The Drum all of the original trilogy, *Floating, Story of A Rabbit* and *360* as well as co-producing in our Lyric Theatre *The Doubtful Guest.*" *Simon Stokes, Artistic Director*

The Theatre Royal Plymouth is the largest and best attended regional producing theatre in the UK and the leading promoter of theatre in the South West. We produce and present a broad range of theatre in our three distinctive performance spaces – The Lyric, The Drum and The Lab – including classic and contemporary drama, musicals, opera, ballet and dance.

We specialise in the production of new plays and have built a national reputation for the quality and innovation of our programme. Our extensive creative learning work is pioneering and engages young people and communities in Plymouth and beyond.

Our award-winning waterfront Production and Learning centre, TR2, is a unique building with unrivalled set, costume, prop-making and rehearsal facilities.

Recent Theatre Royal Plymouth productions include: *The Man With The Hammer* by Phil Porter, *Monster Raving Loony* by James Graham, *The Whipping Man* by Matthew Lopez, *After Electra* by April de Angelis, *Grand Guignol* and *Horse Piss for Blood* by Carl Grose, *Merit* by Alexandra Wood, *Another Place* by DC Moore, *Chekhov in Hell* by Dan Rebellato, *The Astronaut's Chair* by Rona Munro, *Solid Air* by Doug Lucie, and *MAD MAN* by Chris Goode.

The Theatre Royal Plymouth also collaborates with some of the best artists and theatre makers in the UK and internationally. We have regularly co-produced with Ontroerend Goed (*World Without Us, Are We Not Drawn*

Onward To New Era, A History of Everything, Sirens, Fight Night)
Paines Plough (*The Angry Brigade* by James Graham, *Love Love
Love* by Mike Bartlett), Frantic Assembly (*Othello, The Believers*
by Bryony Lavery, *Lovesong* by Abi Morgan) and Told By An
Idiot (*My Perfect Mind, And The Horse You Rode In On*).

We have also co-produced with Complicite (*The Master* and
Margarita, A Disappearing Number), Hofesh Shechter (*Sun,
Political Mother*), Graeae (*The Solid Life of Sugar Water* by Jack
Thorne) and David Pugh, Dafydd Rogers and Kneehigh
Theatre (*Rebecca*). Alongside our own productions we present
a programme of quality and popularity and regularly launch
national touring productions including *Swan Lake* and *Edward
Scissorhands* (Matthew Bourne), *War Horse* (National Theatre)
and most recently *Billy Elliot the Musical.*

For the Theatre Royal Plymouth

Chief Executive	Adrian Vinken OBE
Artistic Director	Simon Stokes
Executive Producer	Victoria Allen
Marketing & Communications Director	Marianne Locatori
Operations Director	Helen Costello
Artistic Associate	David Prescott
Artistic Co-ordinator	Louise Schumann
Interim Head of Marketing	Susan Hill
Head of PR	Anne-Marie Clark

Board of Directors

Chairman	Mr Nick Buckland OBE
Vice Chair	Ms Janie Grace
	Mr Francis Drake
	Ms Bronwen Lacey
	Ms Jane McCloskey
	Mr Paul Woods
	Mr Peter Vosper

Supported using public funding by
**ARTS COUNCIL
ENGLAND**

About THE DUKE

I started imagining this show in May 2013. I was working with the ground-breaking National Theatre Wales on an event including a live show, an audio walk, a pop-up story shop and a gig in the woods, called *Things I Forgot I Remembered.* The whole event was inspired by my childhood memories of living with my family in my home town of Llangefni on the Isle of Anglesey in the 1970s.

During this 'memory project' I re-connected strongly with my mother and my grandmother. They were both very generous and kind influences throughout my childhood. My grandmother was a wonderful socialist, pacifist, baptist who supported the Greenham Common Women's Peace Camp, went on a Pensioners For Peace mission to Russia and delivered Meals on Wheels all around the Isle of Anglesey until she was eighty-three years old. My mother is a lively agnostic who was a volunteer fundraiser for the NSPCC and worked for years with The Samaritans.

The project reminded me of the question – "what sort of person do you want to be when you grow up?" The question seemed as relevant now as it did then.

The deeper I got into memory, the louder the present moment became – the civil war in Syria was raging, there were terrorist atrocities all over the world and climate change was becoming increasingly visible. The real world was unavoidable – however hard I burrowed into my past. I knew then that my next project had to connect us to the increasingly urgent and present needs of the world.

In Autumn 2015 I climbed out of memory and, inspired by my mother and grandmother and challenged by the question, "what sort of person do you want to be?", I started to write *The Duke.* I was becoming increasing troubled by the misery and suffering my friends and I saw in the world every day. I was especially moved by images of innocent children who were victims of war. I wanted to make a show that directly and positively impacted on the plight of child refugees. My conscience needed me to do this – I needed to make sense of the work I was doing as a writer-performer.

As I developed the show, I was delighted by the enthusiasm and encouragement I received from family, friends, audiences, producers, promoters and funders. I have really enjoyed working on this project – inspired by the past and the present to imagine a better future.

As I write this, the country is grieving the loss of Jo Cox MP. Her life, her spirit and her work inspires me more deeply to present this show as often as possible, to raise money and awareness for children refugees. I am moved by her compassion and generosity and find her life to be the perfect answer to the question, "what sort of person do you want to be when you grow up?"

Save The Children

Save the Children are delighted to be in partnership with *The Duke*. Shôn approached us with his project and desire to raise money and awareness for our Child Refugee Crisis Appeal and we're excited by the opportunity.

Save the Children is a humanitarian organisation. Wherever disaster strikes, the aim is to be there, saving lives. Their teams do whatever it takes to reach children in desperate need. In 2015, Save the Children responded to 76 emergencies, delivering life-saving food, water, healthcare, protection and education to three million children.

The charity has also been working with children in the UK since the 1920s. Today, Save the Children continue to tackle child poverty here at home through a range of programmes and campaigns. They want to ensure that every child, whatever their background, has the chance to fulfil their potential.

Save the Children's global workforce is made up of around 25,000 staff, including 17,000 who are employed by Save the Children International, and 8,000 by members. Within Save the Children International, 97% of staff live and work in the country where the programme is being delivered.

As of December 2014, Save the Children UK had 1,122 staff members, mostly based at our London head office, with others located across five UK regional offices and supporting our UK programmes.

They also have 112 specialist staff members deployed internationally to provide emergency humanitarian capacity and technical support to overseas programmes.

As well as our staff, we have over 15,000 UK volunteers, who are a vital force behind our work.

Volunteers form the backbone of Save the Children, running our shops, fundraising and advocating for our cause, organising events, campaigning, and supporting our learning and development work. Their endless reserves of generosity, energy and enthusiasm ensure we can deliver real change for children, both in this country and around the world.

The charity's vision is a world in which every child attains the right to survival, protection, development and participation.

They aim to inspire breakthroughs in the way the world treats children, and to achieve immediate and lasting change in their lives.

In line with our aim of encouraging self-sufficiency and building skills locally, Save the Children employ national staff and involve volunteers wherever possible.

To find out more about Save the Children and to donate, please visit the website: savethechildren.org.uk

Foreword

BY GEMMA BODINETZ, ARTISTIC DIRECTOR,
LIVERPOOL PLAYHOUSE AND EVERYMAN

I don't know what I expected the first time I saw a piece of theatre written by Shôn.

I think it was back in 2006.

I think it was *Floating* performed in the old Everyman theatre here in Liverpool.

I do remember thinking: Oh thank goodness! At last!

Because somewhere in the midst of watching *Floating* I recognized that Shôn, via Hugh Hughes, was doing something I'd dreamt of doing but hadn't been clever or brave enough to do myself. In fact, as I sat there, I realized that this show articulated in itself what I thought theatre, whatever its form/audience/budget should try and do and invariably failed to.

And here it was – a two-hander with a simple set and a seemingly naïve and fantastical tale of Anglesey breaking free from the British Isles. It could have been silly or possibly worse "quirky".

But for me it was potentially life-changing.

I know.

Since *Floating* I have endeavoured to see all of Shôn's work and whenever possible I have tried to bring it to Liverpool. I have sat in the rain in Llangefni, I have queued at Edinburgh, I have watched our audiences leave his shows just to see the looks on their faces and memorably after seeing *Stories From An Invisible Town* I had to dash from the Liverpool Playhouse Studio straight to my office to have a good sob before anyone could see me.

Because …?

Because Shôn's work reminds us how far we have travelled from the possibility of innocence.

Because as we are subtly reminded of that journey, we are inevitably brought close to the knots and the compromises, the hardening of hearts, the shrinking of optimism, the deadening effects of pragmatism and the "informed" assumptions that stop us being open to wonder.

This year Shôn brought *The Duke* to our new Everyman in Liverpool. It's a 400 seater that has won global awards for its design, with a stage that comfortably supports a company of 40 actors and an all-singing and dancing set.

The Duke was performed by Shôn as himself sitting at a table.

But our epic stage was filled.

With a story at once enormous and tiny, honest and fantastical, personal and ubiquitous.

It was about an ornament that gets broken.

It was, as I always find it is with Shôn's work, about love and generosity.

Watching a piece by Shôn is in my experience to come away a little bit chastened, but quite a bit more released.

We go in crab-like and wary and find ourselves delightedly shaking hands with him as we exit.

It's okay to be kind.

It's okay not to be cynical.

And the world is full of tenderness and wonder.

If we're open to it.

Not bad for a night in the theatre.

On stage there is a desk, a chair, a microphone and a set of speakers. On the desk there is a computer, a simple sound mixer and two lamps. The piece should be performable as much in a community centre, a room above a pub as in a theatre space.

The performer operates all the sound from his desk – he runs the whole show – there is no technician or sound operator. (Although the performer is referred to throughout this script as male, the role can also be played by a female performer)

The piece should be delivered in the voice of the performer.

Upbeat music plays as the audience enters.

The performer is by the door of the auditorium, as himself, welcoming the audience into the space, shaking their hands and chatting to them. He needs to be open and generous, without making a play out of it. He wears regular, everyday clothes. Once the whole audience has arrived, he turns off the lights in the auditorium and goes on stage, turns on his desk lamps and sits behind the desk. He looks at the audience and then cues his own music.

Music is used throughout the piece. Each piece has been give a title, however, the choice of music is open. Some audio is also used, made specifically for the performance – details will be included when relevant.

MUSIC: Hello

The performer sits and looks at the audience while this short burst of music plays

MUSIC OUT

ON MIC: Hello, thank you all very much for coming. Thank you for being today's audience for The Duke.

OFF MIC: My name is *(name of the performer)* and, to be clear, that is my real name. I am called *(name of the performer)*. I'm not making it up. That is the name my mother gave me and the name I've held onto ever since. I have absolutely no reason not to use my real name here tonight.

I'm only making a big deal out of this because I am sitting here and you are sitting there – because, of course, this is a performance and right now, in this context, I am the performer and you are the audience. But we all know, don't we, what we really are – we are all just people – simply members of this world, sharing this time on this Earth together, doing the best job we can to stay afloat. That's who we really are

ON MIC: human beings desperate to stay afloat.

OFF MIC: So, I am *(name of the performer)* and I am pleased to meet you all. I am thrilled to be here with you. This is exactly where I want to be and you are the people I want to be with. I can see generosity in all of you. I can see a lot of generosity here. And that feels good. In fact that feels very good.

ON MIC: You are kind and generous people and I'm always happy to see the human capacity for kindness and generosity because I sometimes worry what would happen if there was none.

OFF MIC: I sit in front of you now as a man who's going through change

I'm not the man I was a year ago. I'm not the man I will be this time next year.

I want to tell you a story here today in order to share my recent experience,

ON MIC: of one,

OFF MIC: wondering about the value of what I do

ON MIC: of two,

OFF MIC: feeling disconnected

ON MIC: of three,

OFF MIC: hearing my conscience call to me and not knowing exactly how to respond

ON MIC: of four,

OFF MIC: wondering whether to hold on or let go of my dream

ON MIC: of five,

OFF MIC: realising that my mother is only getting older

MUSIC: Fantasy/Reality

ON MIC: In my story I will be using a mixture of fantasy and reality – I will include real people with real names, as well as real people with made-up names and made-up people with real names, although, ultimately, of course, everyone is a work of fiction lying within the confines of the reality of my narrative. As Luis Bunuel says, "fantasy and reality are equally personal and equally felt and so their confusion is a matter of only relative importance"

MUSIC OUT

OFF MIC: Before I begin the story, I need to give you three bits of background.

ON MIC: First bit of background.

MUSIC: Background

MUSIC OUT

OFF MIC: In 1974 my father bought a Royal Worcester porcelain figure of the Duke of Wellington on horseback for £750 – does anyone know what £750 in 1974 is in today's money?

ON MIC: Anyone know

AUDIO: Anyone Know *(repetition of phrase "anyone know" with music)*

The performer gives time for the audiences to shout out their guesses, responding to them before giving them the correct answer

AUDIO OUT

ON MIC: £8,100.

OFF MIC: There were in fact three other figures made by the Royal Worcester Porcelain Company. They were Marlborough, Washington and Napoleon. My father wanted all four, he wanted the whole collection, but the whole collection was out of his reach financially. They would have cost him £2,800 – that's over £30,000 in today's money. And so he bought one – The Duke of Wellington – which we affectionately called, The Duke. All the figures were manufactured as investments

ON MIC: purposefully created and sold in order to make money for the investor.

OFF MIC: My father was very proud of this figure and so he kept it covered in sponge, in a big box, under his bed. Every now and again he'd say to me, "C'mon *(name of performer)* let's go and have a look at The Duke"…..

MUSIC: Up The Stairs

We'd walk up the stairs, take the box from under the bed and take the sponge out and then we'd look at the Royal Worcester porcelain figure of The Duke of Wellington on horseback…

MUSIC OUT

MUSIC: Duke Appears

MUSIC OUT

Then we'd put it back in the box, cover it with sponge, put the box back under the bed, walk down the stairs, and sit in front of the fire in silence, just listening to it crackle.

MUSIC: Father By Fire

And then, my father would say,

ON MIC: "good investment that *(name of performer)* – that piece of porcelain will be very valuable one day"

MUSIC OUT

ON MIC: Background Two

MUSIC: Background Two

MUSIC OUT

OFF MIC: In 2005 I decided to write a film script. I pitched my story idea in a seminar to a really good film producer called Gavin. Now some of you might think, surely he wasn't called Gavin – that can't be his real name – you're absolutely right, she wasn't called Gavin – Kate didn't want me to use her real name – in fact, it was her idea to call her Gavin.

What I'm about to do now is a real re-enactment of that 2005 pitch to Gavin – he gave us exactly eighty seconds to make the pitch to a piece of music:

MUSIC: The 2005 Film Pitch

ON MIC: The story's central character is an enthusiastic emerging Welsh artist scraping a living together in London. He breaks up with his girlfriend and decides to go back home to the Isle of Anglesey to make an experimental documentary film about the island and the islanders. While he's there, he falls in love with his ex-girlfriend's identical twin sister and asks her to marry him. When he proposes, there is an earthquake. The earthquake causes the two bridges connecting the island to the mainland to collapse. The island floats away from the mainland, into the Irish Sea and sets off on an epic journey. As it crosses the North Atlantic, it hits a storm, which drives it up to the Arctic, where it almost gets stuck. Luckily, it hits the Gulf stream and returns back via Iceland, narrowly missing the Isle of Man, to the exact same position as it started. To celebrate the island's safe return there is a wonderful wedding attended by whales, dolphins and a huge flock of birds. On this journey, our central character not only learns a huge lesson in love and survival, but he also makes an extraordinary documentary film about this incredible geological event.

MUSIC OUT

OFF MIC: Gavin said,

ON MIC: "there's something in this idea. It's a highly imaginative film within a film, a genre-busting hybrid disaster-romcom-doc. It's like When Harry Met Sally, The Towering Inferno, Titanic, The Life of Pi, Man On Wire all rolled into one."

OFF MIC: He was immediately enthusiastic and then said very seriously,

ON MIC: "I'm not going to shit you – it will take a lot of time and effort to get this into shape. It will take tenacity – you will need to be extremely motivated, disciplined and focussed. If you are, then, maybe, and only maybe, there's a very very very slim chance that it might be considered as a possible script for the screen"

OFF MIC: He said if I thought I had it in me, he could help me develop it. And so, for the next ten years, between 2005 and 2015, I wrote sixty-seven drafts.

It completely consumed me. It became all of me – it became my family, the people I love, the place I come from, who I was, who I'd ever been and how I would be remembered.

By the sixty-seventh draft, Gavin said that the script was impossible for me to improve. He said it was, in his opinion, strong enough to be made into a film. He said he'd take it to a woman called Kate, who was in charge of a very well-financed film company, to see if she'd buy it. Kate is not her real name. Her real name is Gavin. Gavin asked me not to use his real name. In fact it was his idea that I call him Kate.

To say I was excited would be an understatement. I was like a mouse in a cheese shop.

Gavin met Kate and then I met Gavin.

ON MIC: "There's good news and not such good news,"

OFF MIC: Gavin said – he always found a positive way of putting things.

ON MIC: "The good news is that Kate does want to buy the script; the not such good news is – she wants you to make some changes first."

OFF MIC: And then he paused and asked,

ON MIC: "Are you prepared to make the changes she wants you to make?"

OFF MIC: Gavin knew what he was asking me. He knew about the sofa we never bought, the broken window we left unfixed and the restaurants we walked on by. He said,

ON MIC: " *(name of performer)*, you have to understand – Kate is an investor and all films need investment in order to be made; at the end of the day, these films are purposefully made and sold in order to make money for the investor."

OFF MIC: I'm not sure how long I sat there. I'm not sure what my face looked like. I'm not sure if I made any involuntary noises. All I remember thinking is, "Is this where the last ten years has brought me?" and wondering, "Who is this Kate?" Gavin asked again,

ON MIC: "are you prepared to make the changes she wants you to make?"

MUSIC: Waiting For An Answer

MUSIC OUT

ON MIC: "Yes," I said, "I'll make any changes she wants me to make." Gavin said,

OFF MIC: "That's great, because if you make the changes she wants you to make, within the time frame she sets, then she will pay you good money for the script."

MUSIC : Background Two

MUSIC OUT

ON MIC: Background Three.

MUSIC: Troubled

OFF MIC: Over the last few years, the truth is, that I have been feeling increasingly troubled by the amount of misery and suffering that we see in the world every day. I've been struggling to keep my head above water and know which direction to swim. I've been troubled by people losing their worlds and feeling world-less. I've been troubled by our world watching another world as if we're not in the same world. I've been troubled by looking at nameless faces looking at us as we look at them. The world is changing my mind and my dreaming is changing too and I can no longer see the world I once saw.

MUSIC: Background Three

MUSIC OUT

ON MIC: Background over. We can start the story

MUSIC: Commence With Story

MUSIC OUT

OFF MIC: It's October 2015. It's a Friday morning. I'm in my studio, sitting at my desk. I'm waiting for the email from Kate which will tell me the changes she wants me to make to the script and the timeframe inside which she wants me to make them. I have made a strong and resolute decision that whatever changes Kate wants me to make, I will make them. Gavin told me that Kate's email will be with me before ten. It is now twenty past ten and I can feel myself getting annoyed that it's late and begin to wonder who this Kate is. I turn the radio on. I hear a report on some refugees who have failed in their attempt to cross the perilous seas between Turkey and Greece. I try to separate my trivial annoyance about the email being late, from my response to the news. The report tells us how many children were on board, the temperature of the water and the likely deal the refugees made with the person who sold them the boat. It makes the point that the value of a space on the boat is set by the amount of money the refugees are prepared to pay for it. Then the email arrives. I look at it and I'm back to being annoyed. I'm really annoyed that the email has arrived while I'm listening to the report on the refugees. I can't believe how disrespectful Kate is being – surely she could have waited until the end of the report before she sent her email. I can't listen to the radio report and read the email at the same time. That simply can't happen. That'd wrong. I wait until the end of the report. I turn the radio off and read the email. Kate says she has attached a document with the changes she wants me to make and tells me that I need to make them all by Friday next week – in seven days time. There are no niceties, no polite, "hope you are well", no, "well done on the script". There's no sight of an apology for her email being late. She's straight down to business. I open the attachment – it's a fifteen page document listing fifty-three changes. Not small changes. They are big changes. I read,

ON MIC: "the central character is not Welsh, he is American".

OFF MIC: The strong and resolute decision that I made to make any changes she wants me to make crumbles like a wall made of sand. Then the phone rings. I look at it. It's my mother. And I think –

I can not not pick up the phone to my mother – my mother is seventy-five years old and always phones for a reason.

I can not not pick up the phone to my mother – since my father died, she has become increasingly precious and has fewer and fewer friends around her

I can not not pick up the phone to my mother, and so I pick up the phone to my mother

MUSIC: Mam Phone

ON MIC: *(name of performer)*, is that you?

Yes, hello Mam. Are you okay?

Oh! *(name of performer).*

What is it Mam?

Oh! *(name of performer).* You won't believe what I've done

What have you done Mam?

I've only just gone and broken The Duke

MUSIC OUT

OFF MIC: I was upset.

I didn't know if I was upset because my mother was upset

Or if I was upset because I knew my father would have
been upset

Or if I was upset because I was upset about the refugees

Or if I was upset because I was upset about the changes
Kate demanded

I didn't know why I was so upset, all I knew is that I was
upset. I was very upset – much more upset than I needed
to be over a piece of broken porcelain.

What had happened is that my mother decided, in 2005,
a few years after my father died, that, "it was ridiculous"
to have the Royal Worcester porcelain figure of The
Duke of Wellington on horseback surrounded by sponge,
in a big box, under the bed. She decided it was a much
better idea to have the figure out, on the table, in the bay
window, where she could enjoy it every day. And so, for
ten years, that's where it stood. And my mother said that
over the three thousand days it stood there it had become
some sort of companion to her and that when it broke she
was surprised by how upset she was. She said that when
it broke, it revealed to her how a quiet sense of loneliness
had crept into her life

MUSIC: Loneliness

What I discovered in that phone call is that since 2005, since my mother had The Duke on the table in the bay window and I'd had my script on my desk, is that I hadn't fully noticed that my mother's life was changing and that, of course, she was only getting older.

MUSIC OUT

I said to my mother, "Steffi isn't here this weekend" – Steffi is my wife – she'd gone to Switzerland, where she comes from, to see her mother – "why don't you come and stay for the weekend". She said,

ON MIC: "I'll be on the 6.48 train"

OFF MIC: I go back to the fifteen page document. I read,

ON MIC: "the central character is a painter – he's gone to the island to paint portraits of the islanders."

OFF MIC: I tried to take this in. A major part of the film was the idea that the central character was making a documentary film – the concept of a film being made within a film was central. I decided to call Kate to talk to her. I checked the email for a phone number – there wasn't one – so I called Gavin. Gavin told me not to call Kate. He told me categorically,

ON MIC: "you make the changes, she buys the script; you don't make the changes, Kate doesn't invest – no investment, no film."

OFF MIC: He reminds me that he told me when we set off on this journey it was always going to be "high risk". I tell him I understand, it's very clear and that I will make the changes. I returned to the script but I couldn't stop wondering who this Kate was and then I started to wonder what the person who sold spaces on the boat to the refugees told them. Was it that simple? "No money, no space on the boat". Did he warn them that the journey was "high risk"? Before I knew it, it was quarter to seven and time to pick my mother up

MUSIC: Run To Bargain Car Hire Place

And so I ran out of my studio, down Kingston Street, across the Mill Road, past the Bargain Car Hire Place where Tony works, and, when I got to the station, there was Gavin.

MUSIC OUT

He asked me what I was doing and then I saw my mother. I panicked – I didn't want Gavin to know that my mother was coming for the weekend and so, as she got closer, I waved to her and said, "Hello Mrs Jenkins, I've just seen your son, Terry, Terry Jenkins – he's having a few problems parking his car – he asked me to tell you he'll be here in just a moment." My mother looks at me. She looks very confused. It's clear she has no idea what I'm on about and says,

ON MIC: "C'mon *(name of performer)*, give us a hug,"

OFF MIC: and I say, "Mrs Jenkins, I'm more than happy to give you a hug, as long as you know that your son, Terry Jenkins, is not here now, but he will be here in a moment," and she said,

ON MIC: "*(name of performer)*, what are you playing at?"

OFF MIC: And I looked up and Gavin had disappeared, and so I said, "I'm just messing about Mam," and she said,

ON MIC: "I don't think I'm ever going to understand you."

OFF MIC: I took her suitcase and we headed home. As soon as we got there, she said,

ON MIC: "Shame Steffi isn't here – c'mon, let's go to the pub and tell your friends to come and join us."

OFF MIC: I didn't take her suggestion to tell my friends we were going to the pub as a sign of anxiety she might have about spending the whole weekend alone with me. I understood immediately that it was her desire to be part of some sort of social gathering. It was company she craved. And so, we went to the pub

MUSIC: Pub Music

There was a real Friday night atmosphere. It was wonderful to see so many friends come out and join us. Inevitably, after a while, a conversation about The Duke opened up. My mother was keen to explain exactly how it had broken. She'd made this

The performer holds up a paper 'diagram' of the figure

She said,

ON MIC: "basically, what happened is, I picked up the horse by its torso and when I lifted it, it just separated from the hooves. The hooves stayed attached to the mound."

OFF MIC: We laughed a bit and then my mother brought this

The performer holds a small yellow nylon brush for dusting

out of her handbag and said,

ON MIC: "this is what I used to dust it."

OFF MIC: My mother's story brought us all a bit closer. And then someone suggested that the next day, Saturday, everyone should go to town on a sort of treasure hunt – to look for a replacement Royal Worcester porcelain figure of the Duke of Wellington on horseback. Everyone agreed and we decided to meet at CB2 Cafe at five o'clock to find out who the winner was. My mother was delighted that her problem had been made into some sort of sport.

MUSIC OUT

It was one of those nights in the pub when the drinking felt like it was part of being together.

It was one of those nights in the pub that lets us into each others lives just a little bit more.

The whole evening was not only an antidote to loneliness, but, also, remarkably, it was an antidote to the ageing process, because, when we left the pub that night to walk home, my mother literally skipped down the street.

MUSIC: Mother Is So Happy

ON MIC: She made this little turn and went up onto her tiptoes. We got to the front door of the house, I opened it and she floated up to bed.

MUSIC OUT

OFF MIC: I sat downstairs in the kitchen with my laptop. I looked at the fifteen page document with the fifty three changes. I read,

ON MIC: "make sure you put an Audi TT Coupe into as many scenes as possible – they are happy to invest".

OFF MIC: I write, "A vehicle carrier crosses the Menai Bridge onto the Isle of Anglesey full of Audi TT Coupes. It hits the curb and swerves. There is a slow motion shot of all different coloured Audi TT Coupes falling off the carrier and down into the Straits below." I stop. I delete what I've written and decide tonight is not the night to make any changes to the script. I close my laptop and turn out the lights downstairs. I realise that the more the world falls into chaos and crisis, the more I love my family and friends, and, as I walk up the stairs, I think of my mother asleep and of Steffi with her mother in Switzerland.

The next morning, my mother and I went to Burleigh Street – an area of Cambridge full of charity shops. She said she knew that winning wasn't important, but, that she'd never won a treasure hunt before and that she'd quite like to win one. She said I should leave things to her. We went into the first charity shop and she said,

ON MIC: "We're looking for a Royal Worcester porcelain figure of The Duke Of Wellington on horseback, have you got one?".

OFF MIC: The question was well thought out and very efficient, but completely threw the shop assistant. My mother asked again,

ON MIC: "we're looking for a Royal Worcester porcelain figure of The Duke Of Wellington on horseback, have you got one?"

OFF MIC: The shop assistant replied. "I don't really know what that is, but you're welcome to look around the shop at your own convenience." And so we did.

My mother found this very small porcelain figure of a
Geisha Girl and she said to me,

ON MIC: "*(name of performer)*, come over here a minute, come
over here, have a look at that. Have a look at that and tell
me – who does it remind you of? Look at it properly. Does
it remind you of you're Aunty Margaret? Does it? You're
lovely Aunty Margaret who did the flower arranging for
your father's funeral. D'you remember? And she wanted
to be paid and I said I didn't think it was appropriate to
pay a family member for arranging flowers for a family
member's funeral and she said it was her job – that her
profession was Flower Arranger and so I paid her. D'you
remember? And a few weeks later she paid me back
because she was embarrassed and so I bought her a bike.
D'you remember? Then she had that terrible accident –
d'you remember – the accident – and the bike was left at
the back of the house to turn to rust. D'you remember? I
think I'll buy it."

OFF MIC: And she bought it for one pound and seventy five
pence.

A couple of shops later, my mother saw a DVD of 'When
Harry Met Sally' and said that ever since I'd told her
that Gavin had said that my film script was a little bit like
'When Harry Met Sally' she'd always wanted to watch it
and so she bought it and put it in her handbag.

A few shops after that, after my mother asked her usual,

ON MIC: "We're looking for a Royal Worcester porcelain
figure of The Duke Of Wellington on horseback, have you
got one?"

OFF MIC: we heard this – "I know that figure. It's part of a
collection of four. There's not only Wellington – there's
also Marlborough, Washington and Napoleon. Truth

is, one on its own is not really worth a lot, but the four together, well, they're still worth a pretty penny y'know". Now, most of you here probably don't recognise that accent – that accent is classic Snowdonia. My mother recognised it and asked the man which part of Snowdon he was from. They got chatting and she found out that he was an off-duty Police Chief who was in charge of a small station in the mountains. He said he was, officially, an 'amateur private porcelain figure collector' who liked using his spare time visiting different parts of the country looking for porcelain figures. There was something about him which reminded me of a bulldog.

Then we bumped into a friend who was in town on the same treasure hunt as us. He told us that in Cambridge there was a road called East Road and on East Road there's an office block called Wellington House and that it's called Wellington House because The Duke of Wellington played real tennis on a court that used to be on the site where Wellington House now stands. This blew my mother's mind.

ON MIC: "We have to go there,"

OFF MIC: she said. It was a Saturday morning, so the office block was closed, but there was a cleaner cleaning the reception. I knocked on the glass door. She came to open it. My mother said to her,

ON MIC: "I know this might sound strange, but my husband, who's dead now, invested in a porcelain figure of the Duke of Wellington on horseback, and we've just found out that he used to play Real Tennis here. Can we come in please and stand in the building for a moment – I just think it'd be lovely if we stood where he played."

OFF MIC: I noticed that the cleaner was concentrating really hard on what my mother was saying, and then she said in a heavy accent,

ON MIC: "I'm sorry for your loss."

OFF MIC: She spoke slowly and deliberately. It was clear that English wasn't her first language. My mother said,

ON MIC: "Don't worry – my husband died fifteen years ago. I'm used to it. It's just I broke this porcelain figure… and… well, can we come in and stand in the building."

OFF MIC: The cleaner opened the door; we went in. Lying on the floor, behind the reception, were two young girls, drawing with crayons. The cleaner asked me if my mother was my mother and if her husband was my father and then she said,

MUSIC : In Silence

ON MIC: "I don't know if my husband is still alive. I am here with two daughters. Their father. He, home. There is war."

OFF MIC: My mother and I stood in silence, not knowing what to say.

ON MIC: "Thank you for letting us in"

OFF MIC: my mother said.

"Not problem." said the cleaner, "have a good day". As we walked away my mother said,

ON MIC: "That was awful. So awful. Poor poor poor woman. I felt like I wanted to give her something."

MUSIC OUT

ON MIC: "I wanted to give her money, then I thought that would just be embarrassing, especially in front of her children and then I thought I could give her the DVD of 'When Harry Met Sally', then I thought that'd be so inappropriate".

OFF MIC: I noticed a black Audi TT Coupe drive past, driven by someone who looked like Gavin.

By now it was five o'clock. We went to CB2 Cafe to meet everyone. No one, unfortunately, had found a replacement Royal Worcester porcelain figure of the Duke of Wellington on horseback – but one friend had found a pair of Wellington Boots – he claimed that was pretty close and that he should be declared the winner of the treasure hunt. Another friend had a video of the 2015 bi-centennial anniversary re-enactment of the Battle of Waterloo with a voice-over in Flemish – she claimed that was closer than Wellie boots. Then my mother took out Margaret, the Geisha Girl and said,

ON MIC: "at least this is a porcelain figure."

OFF MIC: Everyone agreed she was the winner. She was thrilled, even though she knew, deep down, no one had really won. The next day was Sunday

MUSIC: Sunday Yeah!

Me and my mother had a fantastic day – walking, talking, preparing a roast supper together. I asked her about her loneliness and she said,

ON MIC: "listen *(name of performer)*, The Duke breaking was a really positive thing because it made me realise where I am in my life. And I need to attack it. So, when I go back home, I'm going to join the rowing club – you know the one with those four-oared Celtic longboats which go up and down the Menai Straits; and I'm going to go back to playing Bridge, because you know I left because Brian was so annoying, well Brian's passed away – every cloud has a silver lining."

MUSIC OUT

OFF MIC: I have to admit I was really inspired by her approach. Before she went to bed that night she said,

ON MIC: "I don't think I'll watch the news tonight"

OFF MIC: The next day, Monday, Steffi returned home from Switzerland and, I just want to say

AUDIO: Steffi *(a piece of audio about how wonderful Steffi is, starting with 'Steffi is…')*

AUDIO OUT

I love Steffi. I love her more and more and more and I don't want anyone here to think that Steffi made me put that in the show – in fact she said she finds it slightly embarrassing and I told her that was surely half the point. I love Steffi very very much.

Steffi and I walked my mother to the station – Steffi had an appointment in town and left us halfway. As we walked past the Bargain Car Hire Place where Tony works, Gavin stepped out of a black Audi TT Coupe and, before I had a chance to say anything, my mother said

ON MIC: "Oh hello, we didn't get a chance to say a proper hello on Friday did we? Well, I'm Mrs Jenkins and my son is called Terry Jenkins and Terry Jenkins, my son, has got a car and he isn't here today because he is working somewhere that you need a car to get to. So *(name of performer)*, who's not my son, said he'd carry my suitcase and walk me to the station."

OFF MIC: Gavin shook my mother's hand, then looked at me and said,

ON MIC: "Make sure you get an Audi TT Coupe into as many scenes as possible."

OFF MIC: Then he laughed, as if he'd told me one of his favourite jokes. Then he said,

ON MIC: "only one hundred hours to go until the deadline"

OFF MIC: and disappeared.

ON MIC: "What's he talking about?"

OFF MIC: my mother asked. Without thinking, I said, "My script deadline – there are one hundred hours between 1pm today and 5pm on Friday." My mother said,

ON MIC: "Why didn't you tell me you had a script deadline. You shouldn't have spent the weekend with your mother when…right, go to your desk right now and write your script."

OFF MIC: She took her suitcase off me and disappeared through the barriers, then turned and did a little Geisha Girl bow. She made herself laugh. I did a small Geisha Girl bow back to her.

As I walked back to my studio, I passed the cleaner from Wellington House walking with her two daughters in either hand. She saw me and nodded. I waved. One of the girls waved back. I was glad my mother hadn't offered her 'When Harry Met Sally'.

Then I did something I'm sure we all do when you pass someone's window – I had a little peek inside.

MUSIC: Duke Appears

There, on an antique table, in the bay window, stood a Royal Worcester porcelain figure of The Duke of Wellington on horseback. I ran across the road, I knocked on the door. No answer. I knocked a bit harder. No answer. I knocked really hard. Still no answer. I double-checked to see if it really was a Royal Worcester porcelain figure of The Duke of Wellington on horseback and it definitely was. And so

AUDIO: Going Down Side Alley *(a playful audio track set to music about going down the side alley with the intention of stealing the figure)*

AUDIO OUT

I got to the back of the house. I couldn't believe I was prepared to break in, but I kept thinking that my mother would be so pleased if I replaced The Duke. I look through the window. I see a kitchen. I knock on the back door and when I knock, the door opens just a little bit. I put my hand on the door and I push it open.

MUSIC: Walk Into Kitchen

I'm in the kitchen. I notice there's a table with a laptop on it. I shout, "Hello. Is there anyone in?" No reply. Ahead of me, there's a door. I walk towards it and I walk through it into the next room. It's a dining room. There's a dining table with an old man, around the same age as my mother, doing a jigsaw puzzle with his hearing aid beside him.

MUSIC OUT

He looks up and he says,

ON MIC: "Hello, do I know you?"

OFF MIC: I say, "no, no you don't but we do have a friend in common – we both know the Duke of Wellington." He looks really confused. I say, "you have a Royal Worcester porcelain figure of The Duke Of Wellington on horseback in your front room. My mother broke hers recently. I need to replace it. I want to buy it." And then he said,

ON MIC: "I'm happy to sell it to you, but if I sell you Wellington I'll have to sell you all four. You see Wellington is part of a collection – there's also Marlborough, Washington and Napoleon."

OFF MIC: He said that in his opinion a fair price was £4,000 for all four and that he wasn't prepared to negotiate. I knew the collection was worth £2,800 in 1974, over £30,000 in today's money. I said I'd buy all four.

He asked if I banked online and if I had my details. I told him I kept my details on my phone. We went through to the kitchen and we sat with his laptop on the kitchen table. I transferred £4,000 from my account into his account. Then he asked if it was my usual behaviour to walk into other people's houses uninvited. I apologised to him. He said,

ON MIC: "you must love your mother very much."

MUSIC: You Must Love Your Mother

OFF MIC: I said I did.

MUSIC OUT

We went up to his attic to get the three boxes that housed Marlborough, Washington and Napoleon and the box for The Duke. He showed me his wife's wedding dress and said it was one thing he'd never sell, no matter how much anyone was prepared to pay for it. I liked him. I like him a lot. I stayed for a cup of tea. We swapped names. He told me he was called Edward and that when he was younger he was called Bedward – not because he was successful with the ladies, but because he was lazy.

I found myself outside the house with the four big boxes. I see Steffi down the street walking towards me – she sees me – I wave – she waves back. As she approaches, I ask if she can help me carry the boxes to my studio. She balances one box perfectly on top of another and lifts them both up. That might sound simple, but, really, it's not. The boxes are really quite big. Steffi makes it look simple. She's very good at making things look easy. I try to copy exactly what she did. I do manage it, but not with the same sense of ease. The two of us walk down the street carrying the four boxes.

MUSIC: Boxes and Bargains

Steffi asks me what's in the boxes and I don't give her a straight answer. I say, "Stef, you know how my father wanted to buy all four Royal Worcester porcelain figures of military heroes on horseback. And you remember how they were out of his reach financially because they would have cost him, back then, £2,800, which is over £30,000 in today's money. You remember that Stef. You remember that. Well, the thing is Stef, the thing is, and you're not going to believe this, but the thing is, I have just bought all four figures, the entire collection, for a bargain price of

£4,000. I have saved £26,000." By this point we're at my studio. We put the boxes down, next to my desk where my script is and Steffi says to me, "*(name of performer)*, you have not just saved £26,000 – you have just spent £4,000" and I say to her, "yes but Stef, I had to spend the £4,000 in order to save £26,000." Then she looks at me and she says, "perhaps you should concentrate on making those changes to your script," and she leaves.

MUSIC OUT

I sit down and I look at the fifteen page document listing fifty three changes. I read,

ON MIC: "All the scenes at the beach need to be set in a swimming pool. Pools are cheaper than beaches."

AUDIO: Beach To Pool *(an internal monologue about the fact that the majority of the film is about an island at sea)*

AUDIO OUT

OFF MIC: All I could see in my mind was my mother arriving back home and placing Margaret, The Geisha Girl where The Duke stood. I decide – I have to get The Duke to Anglesey.

MUSIC: Run To Bargain Car Hire Place

I ran down the street, towards the Bargain Car Hire Place where Tony works. I got there and I said, "Tony, Tony, I need to hire a car straight away," He said, "I'm really sorry, everything is out at the moment *(pause)* the only car I've got right now is an Audi TT Coupe." "That's crazy," I said. He said, "Normally the Audi TT Coupe goes out at £300 a day, but, I will let you have it, at a bargain price of £230." I look at him and I say, "Tony, £230 is not a bargain. A saving of £70 is not a bargain. I'll tell you what a bargain is Tony. I'll tell you what a bargain is. A bargain is when a man pays £4,000 for four porcelain horses which should cost him over £30,000. It's when a man saves £26,000 on four porcelain horses. That's a bargain. £230 is not a bargain." And Tony said, "well, d'you want the Audi or not." I said, "Yes please." We did the paperwork, we walked across the courtyard and did the checks on the car. As he gave me the keys he said, "Some people consider the Audi TT Coupe to be the height of egocentricity, I say driving one is the closest anyone like you or me will get to feeling like James Bond." I got in and drove off.

MUSIC: Total

Being in that car made me feel different. Being behind that wheel made me feel like I didn't have a care in the world. Looking through that windscreen made the world look like it was there for my taking. An Audi TT Coupe isn't just a car.

MUSIC OUT

I park the car next to my studio. I look at the boxes and I look at the car. I look at the car, I look at the boxes. There is no way the boxes will fit in the car. The boxes are too big. The car is too small. I take The Duke of Wellington, Marlborough, Washington and Napoleon out of their big boxes and line them up on my desk next to the script. And then I see Gavin sitting behind my desk. He says,

ON MIC: "You're making a big mistake. This is a once in a lifetime opportunity you've worked ten years to get. If you like how that car makes you feel, you should make the changes to your script."

OFF MIC: The phone rings. It's Steffi. I explain everything to her and she turns up with bubblewrap and wraps the figures up and straps them into the passenger seat using the seat belt. I say to her

AUDIO: Steffilove *(a short playful audio track set to music about how I love Steffi)*

AUDIO OUT

I get in the car and I drive off to Anglesey.

MUSIC: Set Off To Anglesey

A14, M6, M6 Toll Road, M6, M56, A55. It's a route I'd taken many times before. Everything goes to plan until I come off the M6 Toll Road and see a diversion sign telling me there are major night roadworks ahead.

MUSIC OUT

I make a snap decision, get off the motorway and take the alternative route through the mountains. I put the radio on.

MUSIC: Darker

I listen to a report about a fifteen-year old boy who has made it to Europe from Syria after losing his entire family to war. As I drive into the mountains, it gets darker. The roads get smaller. I slow down. The report informs us about the number of unaccompanied child refugees that live in camps throughout Europe. I notice the petrol gauge is hitting empty. The roads are getting smaller and it's getting darker. The report talks about child sex trafficking. It gets very dark.

MUSIC OUT

The road feels like it's running out, then, in the distance, a small pin-prick of light. A small beacon of hope.

MUSIC: The Wheel of Fortune

A small independent petrol station. The report talks about the work of some relief organisations. It talks about families being re-united. It's a small station with one pump – you can go either side of it.

MUSIC OUT

One side is taken – I take the other side. I get out.

ON MIC: "Nice car"

OFF MIC: says the man filling his car – we're in Wales. "It's not mine" I say. "I nicked it." He laughs.

ON MIC: "What you got in the front their in all that bubble wrap"

OFF MIC: he asks. "Four severed heads, " I say, expecting another laugh. "Okay" he says, "I'm an off-duty Police Chief." And then, of course, I recognise him, he's the 'amateur private porcelain figure collector' we met in Cambridge at the weekend. He looks a bit like a bulldog. He says, "The thing is there have been a number of burglaries in the area recently – I'm afraid I'm going to have to look." I open the passenger door, he unwraps the figures and places them on the bonnet of the car. "Well, if Mohammed won't go to the mountain then the mountain will go to Mohammed – I'll give you £6,000 for them." I tell him I could, possibly, sell him three, but I need to hold onto Wellington. "I'll give you £8,000," he barks. I say "it's not about the money." "I'll give you £10,000," he shouts. I tell him I can't. "I'll give you £12,000," he insists. I explain the situation – how my father bought The Duke as an investment, my mother broke it, got upset and, as I explain, I look at the four figures on the bonnet of the car, under the white light of the petrol station, in the mountains, and I say,

ON MIC: "They're actually worth over £30,000."

OFF MIC: The off-duty Police Chief-slash-'amateur private porcelain figure collector' looks at me as if he's going to rip my head off and says,

ON MIC: "The value of those figures is the amount of money that the buyer is prepared to pay for them."

OFF MIC: And then he looked up at the sky and he howled

MUSIC: Police Dog

And then he walked around the car and climbed onto the bonnet, sniffed the four figures, then came right up to me, dropped down on all fours, barked and bit me. He bit into my calf muscle. It really hurt. I shook my leg to try to get him off. He held onto it. His teeth were sinking into my leg.

MUSIC OUT

Then he stopped, stood up and shouted "You Audi TT Coupe drivers, you drive me crazy." Then he got into his car and drove off.

I paid for the petrol, put the four figures back in bubble wrap and into the car and started the engine. A couple of miles down the road I noticed some blue flashing lights in my wing mirror – I saw two policemen and I thought, "I'm not stopping," and I put my foot down

MUSIC: Escape

I drive really fast. I notice an open gate. I drive through the gate into the fields. The fields are full of mud. There's mud all over my windscreen. I can't see a thing. I put the windscreen wipers on. I'm right at the edge of a cliff. I slam on the brakes. I stop. I get out the car with my hands up. The police car stops behind me.

MUSIC OUT

The two policemen get out. They shout' "Wow! That was fantastic. Nice one! Are the figures alright?" I check them – remarkably, they're unscathed. The policemen take the figures and tell me to follow them to the police station

MUSIC: Police Interview Room

I'm in the middle of a police interview room, in the middle of the night, in the middle of the mountains. In front of me, on the table, unwrapped, are The Duke of Wellington, Marlborough, Washington and Napoleon. Next to them is £15,000 in used notes and the Police Chief holding a baseball bat. He says, "Smell that money – I know you Audi TT Coupe drivers love your money." I tell him the car is hired from a Bargain Car Hire Place near the train station in Cambridge. He looks disappointed and says forcefully, "You take the money; I take these four beauties. You don't take the money; these four beauties become thousands of pieces of worthless porcelain."

MUSIC OUT

I hear the hum of the neon light. I wonder what kind of deal I'm being offered. I wonder what kind of deal the refugees that drowned at sea were offered by the person who sold them a space on the boat. I think about how easily one person can change your entire world. And I wonder who Kate is.

MUSIC: Up The Stairs

I remember going up the stairs with my father to look at The Duke. I say,

ON MIC: "I can't".

OFF MIC: He lifts up the baseball bat, breathes in and pulls it back over his head. I close my eyes. I hear a thud. I open my eyes. The Police Chief is on the floor. The baseball bat is lying next to him. I look at the money. I look at the four figures. I look at him on the floor. I get up and lift the four figures carefully and walk towards the door. The two policemen come in. They look at me with the four figures. They see the money on the table. They look at their Police Chief on the floor with the baseball bat beside him. I can see them looking at the picture like it's a crime scene they need to solve. The Police Chief groans. They make a schoolboy error – both of them run towards him. I run out of the interview room, out of the police station and into the Audio TT Coupe and drive as fast as I can.

MUSIC: Rising

ON MIC: The roads are clear. The sun is rising. The mountains are stunning. I'm in an Audi TT Coupe driving across the Menai Bridge, looking out of the window. Dawn is breaking and the light is bouncing off the Menai Straits. I have a collection of porcelain horses next to me, I can see the Isle of Anglesey ahead of me and I can see the mainland of Wales behind me.

MUSIC OUT

OFF MIC: And then I realise, of course,

MUSIC: This World

> I'm not going back to give my mother The Duke. I'm not
> going back because of a piece of porcelain. I'm going back
> so that she knows I love her and think of her and can't
> put into words what of her. She stands outside the house,
> picking up a bottle of milk. She's surprised to see me –
> even more surprised that I'm stepping out of an Audi TT
> Coupe.

MUSIC OUT

> She says,

ON MIC: " *(name of performer)*, you shouldn't be here, you
should be at your desk, meeting your deadline,"

OFF MIC
> and I say to her, "don't worry about that – I have an
> extension on my deadline." Then I say, "Mam, can you
> go and sit in the living room, I have a surprise for you".
> My mother takes the bottle of milk inside the house while
> I go to get the four figures from the car. I line them up
> outside the living room where my mother is now sitting. I
> shout, "Mam, close your eyes". I pick up the first figure –
> Marlborough – I go into the living room – I stand in front
> of her – I say, "Mam, open your eyes." She opens her eyes
> and she goes

ON MIC: "Aaawwww"

OFF MIC: And I say, "Mam, I'm really sorry, I couldn't find
The Duke, I hope this will do." She says,

ON MIC: "Of course it will."

OFF MIC: Then I see Margaret, the Geisha Girl, standing on the table in the bay window where The Duke used to stand and I see a rowing machine. My mother says,

ON MIC: "that was Brian's – you know Brian who's the reason I stopped going to Bridge – you know I told you he passed away – well his widow gave me his rowing machine – said he'd love me to have it. I have to admit, Life After Brian is definitely better than Life With Brian."

OFF MIC: I say, "Mam, close your eyes" and she says,

ON MIC: "Now look *(name of performer)*, I don't want to be a spoil sport, but I saw you bring in four figures and so I'm guessing you've found The Duke."

OFF MIC: I bring in The Duke

MUSIC: Duke Appears

I unwrap the bubble wrap, and she says,

ON MIC: "… *(name of performer)*…you found The Duke… you…you are a fool…a silly fool….a very silly fool…"

MUSIC OUT

OFF MIC: Then she says,

ON MIC: "You really should have told me you were coming. I had no idea. I have my first session with the rowing club. I can't break the commitment. And, anyway, you need to get back to your desk because I know you were lying about that extension on your deadline. Here…."

OFF MIC: she says and she hands me Margaret, The Geisha Girl.

ON MIC: "Give this to Steffi – I know she'll love it."

OFF MIC: I take it, knowing it's not something Steffi will like one bit. As I say goodbye to her, she says,

ON MIC: "Oh! And by the way, I watched 'When Harry Met Sally' last night – I think that scene in the Deli with the fake orgasm is very very funny."

OFF MIC: She gives me a hug and walks off towards the Straits as I put Margaret in the car. I watch my mother climb into a four-oared Celtic Longboat. I see the refugees climb into their boat. I drive off, back over the Menai Bridge

MUSIC: I Got In The Car

ON MIC: It's the A55, M56, M6, M6 Toll, M6, A14

OFF MIC: As I drive back to my desk, I work out the cost, the financial cost, of this adventure – the cost of the four figures, the cost of the hire car and the cost of fuel and the cost of the M6 Toll Road I'm now on. I do the maths – £4,320.

MUSIC OUT

I check the fuel gauge and decide to stop for petrol, to be on the safe side. I sit in a queue at the petrol station. Margaret is on the passenger seat. A police car pulls up right beside me. Really close. It's him. The car is so close to mine that I can't open the door. He gets out of the police car and marches towards mine. Before I can move, he's there. He grabs Margaret and sits in the passenger seat. He says that Tony at the Bargain Car Hire Place near the train station in Cambridge told him I hired the Audi TT Coupe for a day. He said,

ON MIC: "I knew you'd head back to Cambridge at some point today on this route."

OFF MIC: Then he stops and looks at Margaret, who he's got in his hand. He turns her upside down

ON MIC: "It's a Soviet Porcelain Company Geisha Girl,1929. How much d'you want for it?"

OFF MIC: "£4,320" I say.

ON MIC: "Done,"

OFF MIC: he says, goes to his car, opens a white plastic bag, counts £4,320 in used notes and gives it to me. I hand over Margaret and he drives off. I fill the car with petrol and I get back to Cambridge. I return the car to Tony, I give the money to Steffi and tell her I'll explain everything later. I go to my studio and I sit at my desk.

I sit and I look at the fifteen page document with fifty three changes. I read

ON MIC: "The island the central character returns to is not Isle of Anglesey, it's the island of Manhattan."

OFF MIC: I look at the document for a very long time. I remember sitting by the fire withy my father.

MUSIC: Father by Fire

I think about the last ten years, the sixty-seven drafts. I think about my mother and I think about the cleaner and her two daughters. I think about the investment my father made in The Duke and the value of that Royal Worcester porcelain figure today.

MUSIC OUT

I press Select All, Delete and I write, The Duke, return return, and I start writing.

MUSIC: Motivation

I write all this. I write this show that you have just watched. It makes sense and I feel connected. I don't sleep, I just write and I finish it just before the Friday 5pm deadline and I send it to Gavin and Kate with this letter:

MUSIC OUT

'I've been wondering for a while about the value of what I do. I can't change the world but I can change my script. I've written a live solo show called The Duke, which I've attached. I want to do it for free and ask audiences to donate to The Child Refugee Crisis Appeal run by Save The Children, rather than buying a ticket. It's the only way that I can think of to connect my script to the world that I see at the moment. You might like it – there's plenty of mention of Audi TT Coupes.'

MUSIC: Hello

Ladies and Gentlemen, you might recognise that this tune is the same tune you heard at the beginning of the show and so, in my mind at least, that's a very clear sign that the show is now over. Thank you exceptionally for coming tonight. It has been a real joy being here with you. I can see generosity in all of you. I can see a lot of generosity here. And that feels good. In fact that feels very good.

ON MIC: You are kind and generous people and I'm always happy to see the human capacity for kindness and generosity because I sometimes worry what would happen if there was none.

The performer puts some upbeat music on. He gets up from behind the desk. He walks to the door of the auditorium. He puts the lights back on. He stands by the door with a bucket for donations. The audience exits

Save the Children provide refugee families who have lost everything, with food, water, blankets, tents and medical care. They work to reunite lone children with their families, keep them safe from trafficking and exploitation, provide emotional support, set up safe spaces to play, and help them get back to education.

To help Save The Children reach more child refugees please call 0800 8148 148 to donate by phone.

Thanks for reading the script!

Liverpool, Everyman. May 2016

★★★★
"mesmerising"
The Guardian
(on Floating)

★★★★
"a piece of genius"
The Scotsman
(on Floating)

★★★★
"heartfelt and insightful"
Evening Standard
(on Story of a Rabbit)

Hugh Hughes presents
Shôn Dale-Jones in

The Duke

Produced by Hoipolloi, PBJ Management and Theatre Royal Plymouth

The Duke of Wellington. The Royal Worcester Porcelain Company

visit us at
hoipolloi.org.uk

follow us on twitter
@hellohoipolloi

WWW.OBERONBOOKS.COM

Follow us on www.twitter.com/@oberonbooks
& www.facebook.com/OberonBooksLondon